#LockdownLife

by children & teachers
Compiled by Christina Gabbitas

Authors: Children and Teachers
Illustrator: Michael Bourton
Copyright: Poems & Pictures Ltd

Copyright of poems belong to authors listed in the contents page. The moral right of authors/illustrator have been asserted.

No part of this publication may be reproduced, stored in or introduced into a retrieval system, or transmitted, in any form, or by any means (electronic, mechanical, photocopying, recording or otherwise) without prior permission of the publisher. Any person who does any unauthorised act in relation to this publication may be liable to criminal and civil claims for damages.

A CIP catalogues record of the publication is available from the British Library. ISBN: 9781916254251

Proceeds from book sales to Children's Literature Festivals charity: 1182143 England & Wales.

Children's Literature
FESTIVALS

Published by Poems & Pictures Ltd
Compiled by Christina Gabbitas
Editor: Rebecca Thomas, RM Language Services
Front cover illustration: Ursula Hurst

All the poems in this book are the work of the authors, and no words have been changed in the process of compiling this book.

www.poemsandpicturespublishing.org

#LockdownLife
by children & teachers
Compiled by **Christina Gabbitas**

Cover illustrated by **Ursula Hurst**
Poems illustrated by **Michael Bourton**

About the book

Author Christina Gabbitas put this initiative together to give her purpose in lockdown, as all her school visits and events were put on hold or cancelled. She wanted to give children and teachers the opportunity to pen how they were feeling in lockdown, and to share this with others.

Christina called upon a number of individuals to act as judges, who she has met on her journey over the past few years, including the wonderful actress Jenny Agutter, musician Michael Bradley of The Undertones, and entrepreneur and businessman Dr Stephen Fear, who are all patrons of the Children's Literature Festivals charity (charity number 1182143, England & Wales).

All judges can be found in the acknowledgements at the back of this book.

A special mention goes to PC Stephen Croshaw of Warwickshire Police for all his support.

All published poets receive a free copy of the book, and any further proceeds from sales of books are donated to the Children's Literature Festivals charity

Children's Literature
FESTIVALS

(charity number 1182143, England & Wales).

A huge thank you also to all who have volunteered their time to judge, and a special thanks to poet and illustrator Michael Bourton, who has donated his time to illustrate many of the poems.

Contents

Lockdown Spell Oliver Klumpler p9
Judges' winning choice

Stuck Inside Alessia Centanni p11

COVID-19 Harriet Coates p12

Evening Walks Gill Parr p13

Social Distancing Poem Mohammad Uddin p15

A Verse About a Virus Jennifer Stewart p16

Once Upon a Time in Lockdown Harry Carter p17

School's Out Ruby Naik p18

My Lockdown Poem Eliana Milner p19

Isolation Olivia Webb p21

My Lockdown Poem Emilie Rowe p22

A Sign of the Times Lucia Jesson p23

Carry On Sam Gaynor p25

Quarantine Harshini Ramalingam p27

Poem About Lockdown Phillip Amushan p29

Coronavirus Realisations Lottie Eatherington p30

Lockdown Life Esther Alford p31

Standing in Your Garden Lily Rose p33

Silence in the Courtyard Abdullah Shaker p36

Protect the NHS Emma Donovan p37

The Creation from Isolation Chloe Carter p39

Trapped Ros Kingcome p41

Our Heroes Chloe Bower p43

A Change in Life Nana Baffoe Osei-Sarkodie p44

Coronavirus William Kennedy.. p45

Flickers in Darkness Elise Scotney p47

Lockdown Flora Jacoby Richardson p49

Coronavirus Kaja Dowsett p51

Lockdown Emily Dashwood p52

Ghost Town Cassie Clarence p53

The Predator India Boorman p55

What I Didn't Do in Lockdown Yasmine Ollerenshaw p57

Days Upon Days Slip Away Tamisha Newell p59

The Unravelling Thoughts Deekshita Bathula p61

Stay Home Laila Emmett p62

Despite All the Sadness Lauren Irons... p63

Lockdown Pain Donna Craig p65

Stuck Inside Ruby Hoath p66

You Called Miami Mae Holness... p67

Quarantine Adventures Charlotte Eliza Gunning......................... p69

Sad Amira Collins p70

I Would Violet Drabble... p71

Lockdown Abi England... p72

School Amber Zaman p73

Hey! Georgina Agate p74

Coronavirus Katie Battams p75

Lockdown Sophie Baker p76

Heroes Cohan Burnham p77

Change Rachel Pugh p78

A New Normal Jessica McAndrew-Woods p79

Lockdown Poem Ayla Cheesman p80

When It's Over Ania Mahi-Moutih p82

Locked Down, This Town Olive Felstead p83

Kindness Gabriel Richardson p84

Quarantine Time Nihal Bathula p85

We All Stayed at Home Isabella Hickman p87

The Moments We Miss Scout Wyatt p88

Silence Elaine Brandon p89

Coronavirus Zachary Symonds p90

Since Lockdown Began Thea Markus p91

Trapped Inside Josh Crabbe p92

Not Over Yet Michael Bourton p93

Lockdown Spell

by Oliver Klumpler - age 10

Double, double toil and trouble,
Fire burn and cauldron bubble.
Sleeping in my quiet room,
Chatting to my friends on Zoom.
School work done at kitchen table,
Plugging iPads into cables.
Daily dog walks through the park,
Endless hours of *Baby Shark*.
Bouncing on the trampoline
In between our hours on screens.
Learning all the TikTok moves,
Even though Dad disapproves.
Stuck indoors with Mum and Dad
Slowly going raving mad.
Fighting sister, petting dog,
Watching tadpoles turn to frogs.
Double, double toil and trouble,
Fire burn and cauldron bubble.

Stuck Inside

by Alessia Centanni – age 12

Stuck inside,
Nothing to do,
So bored and tired,
Just like you.

Corona has hit,
Everything has changed,
Nothing's the same,
It's so very strange.

Always be smart,
Stay two meters apart.
Spreading fear across the nation.
Everyone's forgotten about deforestation.

But take a look at the bright side,
There are many facts we can say with pride.

Lockdown is healing global warming.
Many more bees seem to be swarming.
The problems we all thought
Seemed so massive,
But now they are so tiny,
Like they burnt into ashes.

So when things get tough,
There is no need to huff.
Stay safe, stay inside.
Always remember,
We are all in this together.

COVID-19

by Harriet Coates - age 10

COVID-19 was on its way,
COVID-19 seemed here to stay.
COVID-19 *please* go away.
In the year of 2020.

Friends were separated because of you.
The pandemic meant we had nothing to do,
School closed, I miss my teachers too.
In the year of 2020.

My parents' wedding was cancelled, we shared a few tears.
When will it happen, in a few years?
Please COVID-19 disappear.
In the year of 2020.

I miss my family and friends to hug,
But we can't do that because of this nasty bug.
Why can't we just pull the plug?
In the year 2020.

COVID-19, you make me sad.
People are dying, it makes me mad.
Dying alone is very bad.
In the year 2020.

2020 you haven't been fun.
Let's hope this pandemic is nearly done.
We will get through this, each and every one.
In the year of 2020.

Evening Walks

by Gill Parr – Teacher

The deer peers out from behind sun-dappled trees,
Relieved that the rush of day walkers has subsided.
It cocks its ear to listen for our careful steps,
As we approach this most timid of creatures.
We stand together with bated breath.
Its head turns to the side as it sniffs at the twilight air,
Searching for assurance that we are a safe pair of hands.
Cautiously it approaches and allows us a view,
Before loping off into the sunset.
We sigh and continue,
Satisfied with our lot.

Social Distancing Poem

by Mohammad Uddin – age 13

We're turning off the radios,
We've given up on the news,
All this talk about coronavirus,
It's given us the blues.

But life isn't all too bad,
Spending time with all the family.
But sometimes they get on your nerves
And make you storm off angrily.

Doing school from home,
It just isn't for me.
Not having my friends around,
It's really hard you see.

We're turning off the radios,
We've given up on the news,
All this talk about coronavirus,
It's given us the blues.

No one knows much about it,
The virus found an open window.
But hopefully next time,
We'll find some more info.

Staying away from people,
It takes a lot of resistance,
Talking to people
From a really far distance

We're turning off the radios,
We've given up on the news,
All this talk about coronavirus,
It's given us the blues.

A Verse About a Virus

by Jennifer Stewart - age 8

Coronavirus is not so great.
It's hard not being able to see my mates.
But I know lockdown is not a bad thing,
It protects us from the illness the virus can bring.

The time I've spent in lockdown with my family
Has mostly made me feel happy.
We've been on walks, and splashed in the stream,
And all enjoyed watching *The A-Team*!

I was worried about my nanna being on her own,
But now she can visit us in our own home.
We still enjoy family quizzes on Zoom
And look forward to when we can all be in the same room.

We say thank you to the workers that are key,
To the people that are looking after our country.
It makes me sad to hear that people are still dying,
And that their loved ones left behind are crying.

I thought that staying at home would be cool,
But now I really want to go back to school.
I can't wait to have to get through the gates on time,
Hang up my coat and form a neat class line.

Overall lockdown has been good to me.
Still, I can't wait to hug my friends and family.

Once Upon a Time in Lockdown

by Harry Carter – age 13

Once upon a time in lockdown,
London turned into a ghost town.

Working from home,
School from home,
Can't we be anywhere else from home?

Online this,
Online that,
I'd much rather have a face-to-face chat.

People get a cat,
People get a dog
To come with them on their official daily jog.

No toilet roll,
Not even flour,
And although you have the time,
You don't have the will power
To order it online.

You need something new,
Something that you haven't seen before,
Beyond your home or next door.

Confined to our homes,
Doing our own things,
And then the doorbells rings
For the third time today.
You open your door
And there's a parcel on the floor.
The driver's already gone
To deliver the next one.
And now this day will be repeated
Until lockdown is completed.

School's Out

by Ruby Naik – age 13

No school for the rest of the week;
All I heard were excited shrieks.
No more early mornings,
Hardly even a warning.

No school until next Friday,
At home we will stay.
Do not meet your friends.
Give your hands a cleanse.

No school until the Easter term,
Rising numbers for the germ.
Two metres apart,
Not seeing your friends, that is the worst part.

No school until September.
What is it like? I don't even remember.
Overwhelmed with work.
Siblings are jerks.

It isn't as fun as we hoped.
Instead we are up early,
In our houses all day.
Our brains are not in the right way.

My Lockdown Poem

by Eliana Milner – age 10

On March the 23rd,
I felt like a bird
Trapped in a cage
When everything changed.

I was not ready for this summer
When our freedom did a runner.
I was stuck at home
With three books on loan.

I was bored as every day went by.
I felt upset, but I did not cry.
I felt worried and scared towards the beginning,
Towards the end that feeling was dimming.

My country, my town, we were all affected,
Relying on each other to keep us protected.
The world was pretty much shut down,
No adults or children wandering around.
Many thousands of people were infected.
Fortunately our devices kept us connected.
I spent time helping and doing good,
In awe of Captain Tom and his knighthood.
Remember to stay two metres away.
You can still meet in the park to play.
Don't forget your gloves and mask,
It really is not a big ask.
One day coronavirus will stop being a threat,
We'll wash our hands, but we won't fret.
Hopefully soon we will be free,
And people will see … a happy me!

Isolation

by Olivia Webb – age 14

I look out my window and there is not a soul on the street.
I long to see my friend, but I know we cannot meet.
Somebody walks past me.
My natural instinct is to greet them and say hello,
But instead I check my distance and look at my shadow.
Am I two metres apart from them?
Am I too close?
These thoughts all cross my mind and then I freeze.

I hear a knock at the door and I instantly know it's not for me.
And there I stand all alone with nothing to see.
I wake up every morning longing to see a familiar face,
One I knew from when everything was in the same place.
It doesn't have to be this way I whisper to myself,
But then I think of those I endanger when I'm out and about.

Here I stand, tall and proud of those who are working on the front line.
Every Thursday I wait in anticipation to bang a pan that makes a chime.
No one knows what the near future holds,
But I'm sure soon everything will unfold.

My Lockdown Poem

by Emilie Rowe – age 13

It can be hard, it can be tough, however, it's for the ones we love.
Missing grandmas and grandads,
Queuing two metres apart at the supermarket,
Spending birthdays at home.
It can be hard, it can be tough, however, it's for the ones we love.

Online school,
Staying at home,
Face Timing friends when we feel alone.
It can be hard, it can be tough, however, it's for the ones we love.

No hugs from people who aren't in your house,
Hearing the deaths rise,
Hoping your family and friends stay safe.
It can be hard, it can be tough, however, it's for the ones we love.

The deadly virus coming to find us.
It's a beast, like a tiger, attacking its prey.
The cough you never want to hear.
It can be hard, it can be tough, however, it's for the ones we love.

Eight p.m. Thursday night we clap for our workers to make moods bright.
Mum sheds a tear as we see our neighbours from a distance.
It can be hard, it can be tough, however, it's for the ones we love.

A Sign of the Times

by Lucia Jesson – age 14

At times like these it is strange,
We all just wish for a change.
Each day being repeated,
Online work to be completed.
Stuck between four walls,
Only being able to communicate through calls.
Communities helping one another along,
Families keeping each other strong.
Rainbows in windows to show love and support.
No more planes departing from the airport.
Social distancing to stop the numbers from rising.
Keeping fitness up by daily exercising.
Always waiting to hear what Boris has to say.
Remembering those who have passed away.
Eight p.m. clap to say thank you.
Together we will get through.
Stay alert, control the virus, save lives.

Carry On

by Sam Gaynor - age 12

Seedlings still grow,
You can still feel the breeze.
The fields are ploughed
And the sun is still rising.

Breakfast is made,
Then lunch is served.
Dinner is cooked,
Then the evenings unfold.

Sounds are still made:
The chime of a bell,
The crunch of gravel underfoot,
The click of a lock.

Trapped inside,
Not allowed out,
The mind fills up with gloom.

But no matter how bad, how dire, how sad,
The earth still revolves
And life still moves on.

Quarantine

by Harshini Ramalingam – age 11

A siren wails wildly off in the distance,
While I brush my teeth and get ready
For another day of tedious quarantine.
My mum taps away on her computer,
Signalling the time for me to go and feast on food.

Dad brings breakfast for me.
I haven't taken notice of the meal,
Of scrumptious sandwiches and wandering water.
My stomach rumbles in reply,
And that was enough to say 'goodbye'.

After playing some video games, I take a break,
So I go and start my paint-by-number.
My brush gently colours the crystal-white paper,
The colours illuminating the tiger's face.
Oh, what a masterpiece a multicoloured tiger could be.

Lunch is served up
And what a delight - it's my favourite -
Indian-style rice, with some spicy sambar,
Enough to fill up a tummy for the next five hours,
A fact that could help me study for the rest of the day.

The clicking continues,
Though I would rather do something else.
So I go outside and ride my bike,
Enjoying nourishing nature at its best,
Though I'm occupied thinking of the everlasting, blood-curdling combat.

This war is unlike any other,
A foe with no fears other than happy people and zero tears.
Courageous souls will thrive and bring the world some pride.
Whilst we are losing many on the intense battlefield,
You must remember that this conflict is for the good of the future.

Poem About Lockdown

by Phillip Amushan – age 13

Right now, we are all stuck in lockdown
And we have seen the city turn into a ghost town.
And now we are all wondering how long
Until we can finally leave our house to go around.

The virus has got us staying inside;
Lots of us are sulking because we feel so confined.
But the rules have been assigned
And as citizens we need to abide.

I miss the constant gentle breeze of the air,
I miss the way it combed my hair.
At that moment, I wouldn't want to be elsewhere.
Now we are stuck at home, it is not fair.

But now lockdown is starting to ease off
And less people are getting that cough.
Some sports are starting to kick off.
Now, slowly, things will start to cool off.

Ultimately, lockdown has not been the best.
When I first heard about it, it took a moment to digest.
I could wake up when I wanted to,
It all seemed too good to be true.
But then there was a colossal rise in deaths.

Coronavirus Realisations

by Lottie Eatherington – age 15

Time ticks by. Slower and yet
Faster too. I finally have time
To think and to learn and
To reflect on how the world is.

I reflect on my privilege,
I reflect of my doubt,
I reflect on the social media blackout,
And the people who just use the movement for clout.

Lockdown left me sleeping,
Safe in my house. I had no
Fear, for while I slept,
I knew that I would be kept

Safe and protected.
And that is my privilege.

I've done my best with
The time I've had. I got involved,
For once, like I never have
Before; my excuses, I know, were petty.

The fact that I could choose my
Involvement, my hand. I could
Guarantee that I could win,
Because of the privilege of my skin.

But I have chosen to wake up.
I won't play blind, I won't back up. I will help to make things better
And I won't give in. Because, Black. Lives. Matter.

Lockdown Life

by Esther Alford - age 9

Limiting,
Odious,
Catastrophic.
Keyworker heroes.
Devastating,
Once in a lifetime,
Worrying,
Never-ending.

Learning at home,
Indoors,
Family time.
Esther's lockdown life.

Standing in Your Garden

by Lily Rose - age 8

The moon is as big as a hard, rocky boulder.
I look at it and remember that I am not alone.
A hairy hedgehog is lurking in the wet grass.
It reminds me that I have company.
An oval-faced owl is hooting loudly in a dark tree.
It adds noise to my quiet day.
The curious cats are playing mischievously like children.
They give me something to watch, so I don't feel bored.
The tough dogs are barking brilliantly at the fiery fireflies.
They remind me that soon I can run outside with them.
The clever children are naming the shining stars,
Ready to tell their teachers when we are finally back at school.

Silence in the Courtyard

by Abdullah Shaker – age 14

Remember silence in the courtyard?
Remember silence in the street,
Waiting for the biggest fool in England who is just about to speak?
But you wait,
And you wait,
But you can't hear a sound,
For the biggest fool in England has yet to be crowned.
The biggest fool around just cannot be found.

You look out the window,
Hoping for just a sigh,
One laugh,
One word,
One baby's wailing cry.
Wishing that one man, woman or child
Would just walk by.
Alas your wish does not come true,
Not one person strolling along the avenue,
Not one old lady walking her little cockapoo,
No joggers pushing that last mile or two.

I wonder what could inspire fear like this?
No sign of life, just like the Blitz,
Be it monsters, soldiers, beasts or pirates.
Unfortunately, the answer is
Coronavirus.

Protect the NHS

by Emma Donovan – age 13

I don't see the point.
Never will you hear me say
I am happy staying at home,
Because
I don't want to protect the NHS.
And never will I say,
I am not going to see my friends, I will see them every day.
I will never say,
Washing my hands all the time,
Because I am
Always going outside.
You won't see me
Doing online school,
Because I will probably be
Going on a road trip with my friends.
Never will I be
Protecting the NHS.

Now read it backwards.

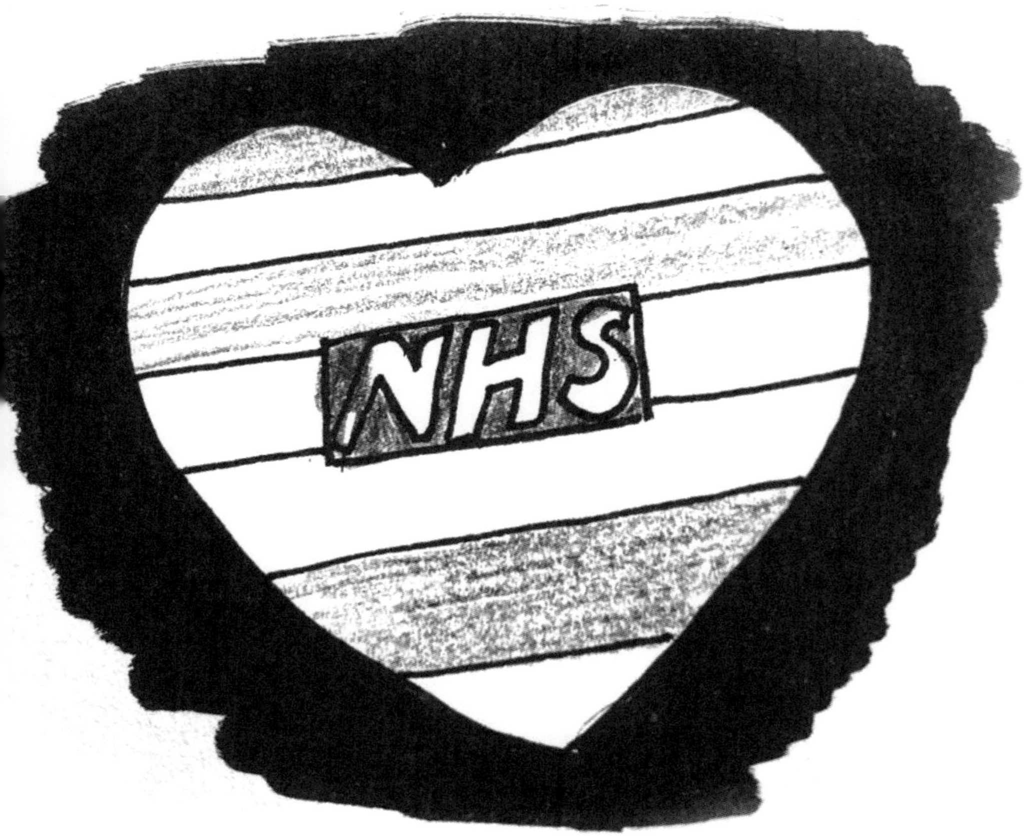
NHS

The Creation from Isolation

by Chloe Carter - age 15

Nice warm breeze on a summer's day.
Kids still going out to play,
Phone in hand, ice pop in the other,
Waiting to get shouted at by their mother.

Tired eyes on a Monday morning,
The English work quickly dawning.
Sitting inside listening to the garden bird.
Checking the news, seeing if people are cured.

Many other houses are better than ours,
All big and tall and covered in flowers.
But my estate is proper dirty;
You should see the family from number thirty.

It's not all like this though.
Better houses than this,
Better streets than this,
All neater than this.

But everyone is working together.
Footballers at home without a bother.
Doctors and nurses helping one another,
And teachers working tirelessly encourage each other.

Communities out praising the work at night
And stars in the sky still shining so bright.
Working from home with a positive hindsight
For the world to come together and put up a fight.

So yes, this is Britain.
And yes, this is one nation.
And as crazy as we are,
We have got through this so far!

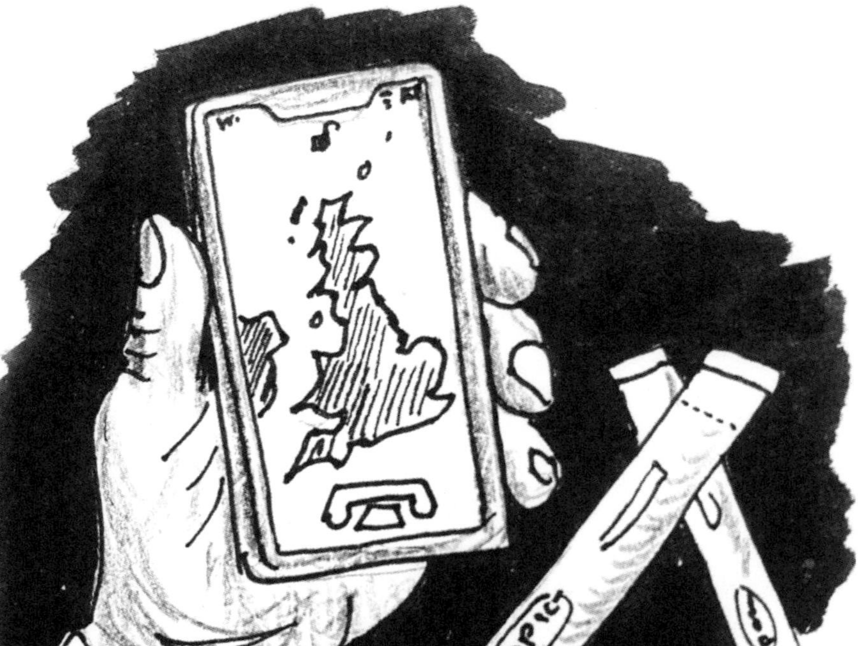

Trapped

by Ros Kingcome – age 12

Trapped in a barred cell,
Fifty blocks high,
No way to escape,
No people to meet,
No places to go.

The world is a dark lonely place
With no room for joy,
Driven by longing.

Freedom is so close,
Yet so far.
You reach out to grab it, but it slips through your fingers, up and away.

Gaze to the sky,
Let your mind run and imagination take you on a journey
To a place you never thought you would see,
Of happiness and joy,
Where you live in harmony.

Then you're back in reality,
So cold and so alone.
The walls are breathing,
Suffocating,
Whispering.
You will never see the light of day again,
Hope is gone.

The clouds are not lonely,
High up in the sky,
So wild,
So willing,
So free.

If only you had held on just a little longer;
Good things come to those who wait.

42

Our Heroes

by Chloe Bower – age 12

There is fear,
There is isolation,
There is sickness,
There is panic,
There is uncertainty,
There is even death.
But,
There is community,
There are blue skies,
There are heroes,
There are fighters.

Amongst all the pain and sadness, we get through it
Thanks to the NHS.
They are our heroes.

A Change in Life

by Nana Baffoe Osei-Sarkodie – age 12

Life in lockdown
Splitting us apart.
I did my morning jog, but it still wasn't enough.
I missed my friend,
All the jokes and the laughs.
I thought it would be good,
I didn't know it would be that bad.

All schoolwork I got online,
I couldn't keep up and do all mine.
But never mind,
The teachers were helpful,
Supporting us to fulfil our potential.

At eight p.m. we will go outside,
Clap for the NHS to make them smile.
Their support is taken in deepest thanks,
Risking their lives for strangers they don't know.

But then time went by,
The lockdown was eased, and some schools opened.
But not mine,
I was stuck in my house like a little mouse.

Sometimes I will go to the park,
Meet a couple friends. I am grateful for that.
Try to write a poem and make someone smile.
It won't be that hard, just believe in yourself.

Coronavirus

by William Kennedy - age 13

Coronavirus, how toxic can it be?
Engulfing all signs of light,
Not to mention team GB!

The earth stood still
And life was sparse.
Never before had I seen such silence,
A calm that stretched out for miles,
Sweeping away the fossil fuels,
Sweeping away the pollution.
The earth stood still.

NHS, you have served us well,
Through all the downs
And ups.
Your guidance has lit a spark.
The community applauds
And salutes you!

The earth stood still and
Life stood empty,
Day after day,
Night after night.
Stay inside, wash your hands,
Make sure you do what's right.

So then COVID,
You think you can take away our dignity?
Well, not this time.
We can get through this
No matter what they say.
We are Great Britain.

No way,
No way will we let this virus take hay from our horses,
Take the fun from our children.
No way.

We can fight this virus.
So, if healthy you want to be,
Then staying home is the key.

Coronavirus.

Flickers in Darkness

by Elise Scotney - age 15

I do not feel the sunset's pull,
Nor do I hear the crooning of day.
I have plucked the stars from the sky
And cast them above me to light the way.

The world seems coiled in a mass of emotion,
Always teetering 'twixt hopes and fears.
The cries of strength echo around,
But never quite land on my ears.

Instead, I hear the hum of night.
Indeed, content with my painted sun,
I listen to the sound of silence, to whispers
Of futures and dreams I could race, but not outrun.

I press myself against a wall, indebted to its soft embrace.
I look upon my callouses, brighter now that I know
That I am enough to scatter the shadows
And I can bring the summer's glow.

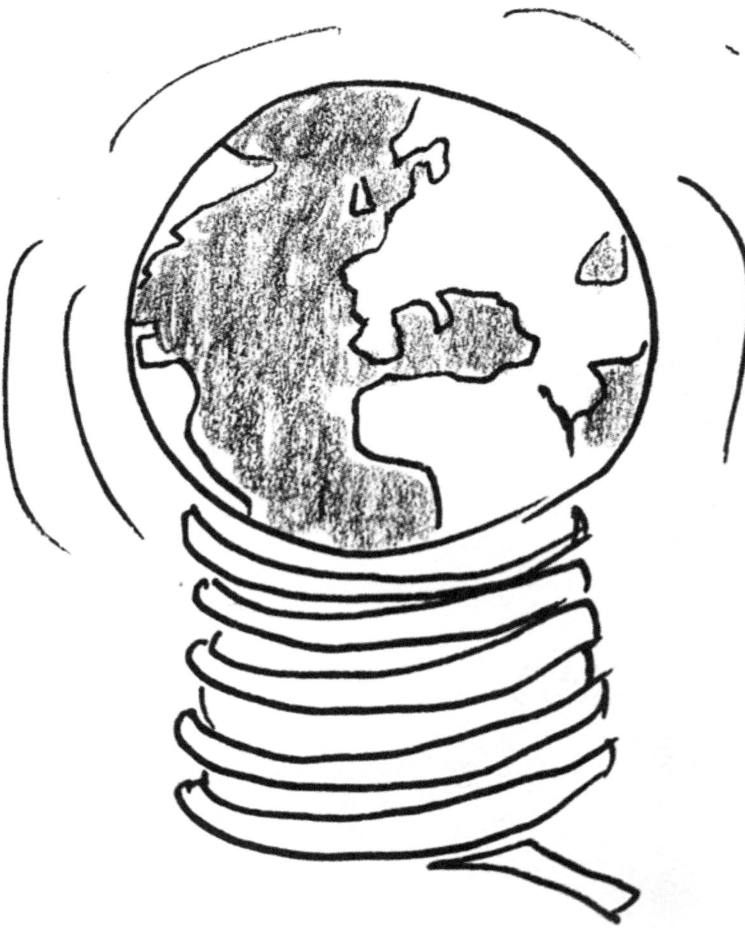

Lockdown

by Flora Jacoby Richardson – age 9

Lockdown, lockdown, I hate it so much.
We're living life like we're trapped in a box.

We can't go out because my parents are busy.
It makes me feel quite a bit grizzly.

I watch TV all day and feel rather drowsy.
Then I go to bed, but tiredness leaves me.

I want to go back to seeing my friends,
making up games, hoping break-time never ends.

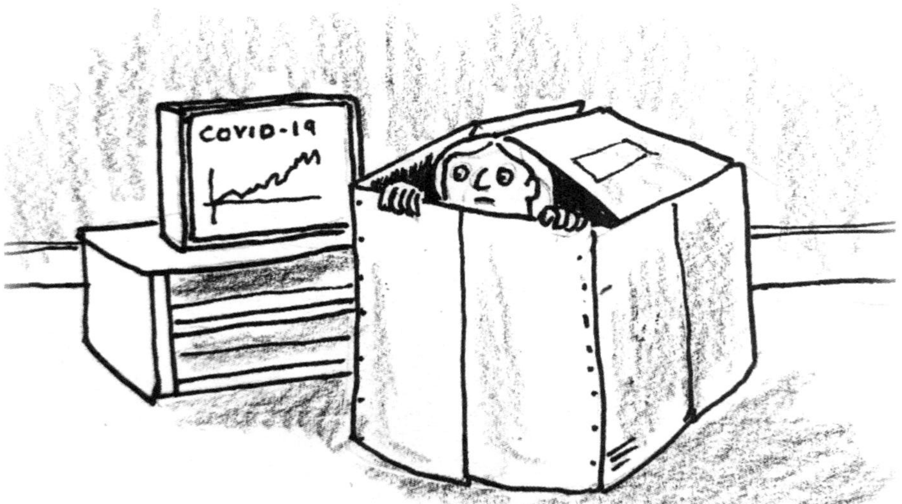
COVID-19

Coronavirus

by Kaja Dowsett– age 13

I'm good for the environment,
Yet people seem to hate me.
It's not my fault you spread me though,
But now you run from me for safety.

I would not have killed these people
If I was not set free.
It was humans who took me out of bats
And you can't blame that on me.

You're so cruel to the environment,
At least I'm giving it a break.
You can't fly because of me,
So there's less carbon intake.

The vulnerable are locked inside,
Watching life as it passes them by.
They clap on Thursdays for those who really shine,
Those who fight me upon the front line.

Think of all the things that I have seen,
Of all the places that I have been.
Think that actually, in the end,
I am what's reuniting the world again.

Lockdown

by Emily Dashwood - age 10

The parents are letting children do anything.
Then there are the kids that do not have siblings.

All the technology is making people crazy,
All the children are getting really lazy.

The coronavirus started this.
All your family you are going to miss.

The NHS are saving people's lives.
You are only allowed to gather in groups of five.

All the walks are making you tired.
All those people are getting fired.

The rainbows are giving everyone smiles.
Playing street hopscotch on colourful tiles.

Home-schooling is really boring
And people are doing lots of exploring.

People are standing two metres apart.
I hated this right from the start.

I hope scientists find a cure
And we won't be locked in anymore.

Ghost Town

by Cassie Clarence – age 13

The virus is stealing lives,
The never-ending whirlwind of deaths –
We are dropping dead like flies!

Be quiet. Keep clean. We are in quarantine.

An invisible enemy, the silent killer
Bringing our world to a shuddering halt.

Be quiet. Keep clean. We are in quarantine.

Welcome to the panic room.
Sheltered behind concrete walls,
We are wondering, waiting, watching – tick tock tick.
Stuck, confined, nothing left behind.

Be quiet. Keep clean. We are in quarantine.

Eerie silence prowls the street –
We do not know when we will meet.
The virus will not win.
We are in this together!

Be quiet. Keep clean. We are *all* in quarantine.

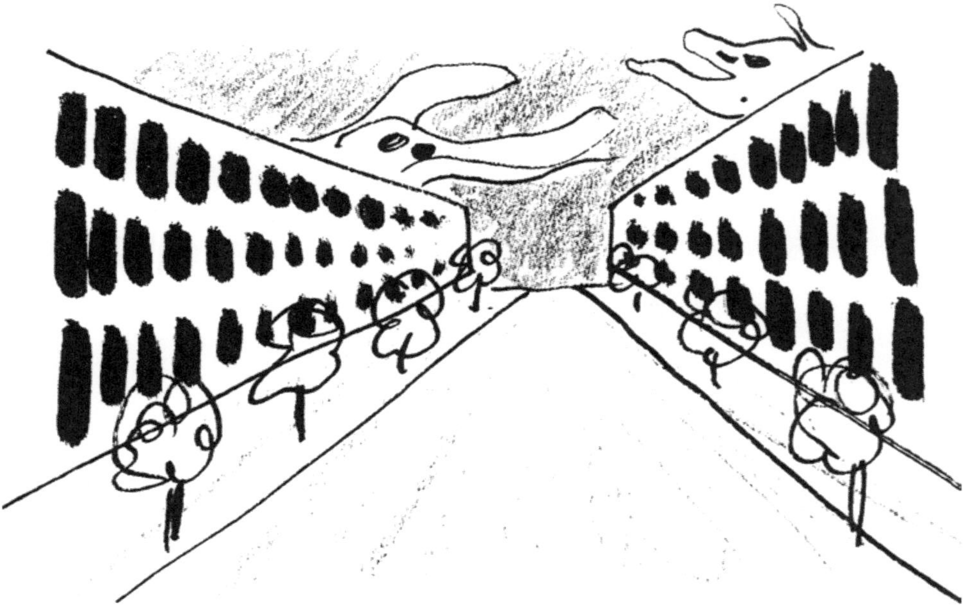

The Predator

by India Boorman – age 13

COVID-19 pounced on our earth.
It silently slithers between our fingers
And now the hope to remove it with soap no longer lingers.
The near predator is merely a coward
And our NHS are the heroes.

The fear its saucer-like eyes will choose me,
Its hunger healed when it feeds on me.
Nature's weapon used on me.
But the near predator is merely a coward
And our NHS are the heroes.

We use vaccines to kill off the virus.
We make sure we have life
And it has death.
We are killing everything in our path
To make sure we survive.
We are the poachers
Murdering the enemy.
The near predator is merely a coward,
But our NHS are the poachers,
And so are we.
Are you sure we're not nature's predator?

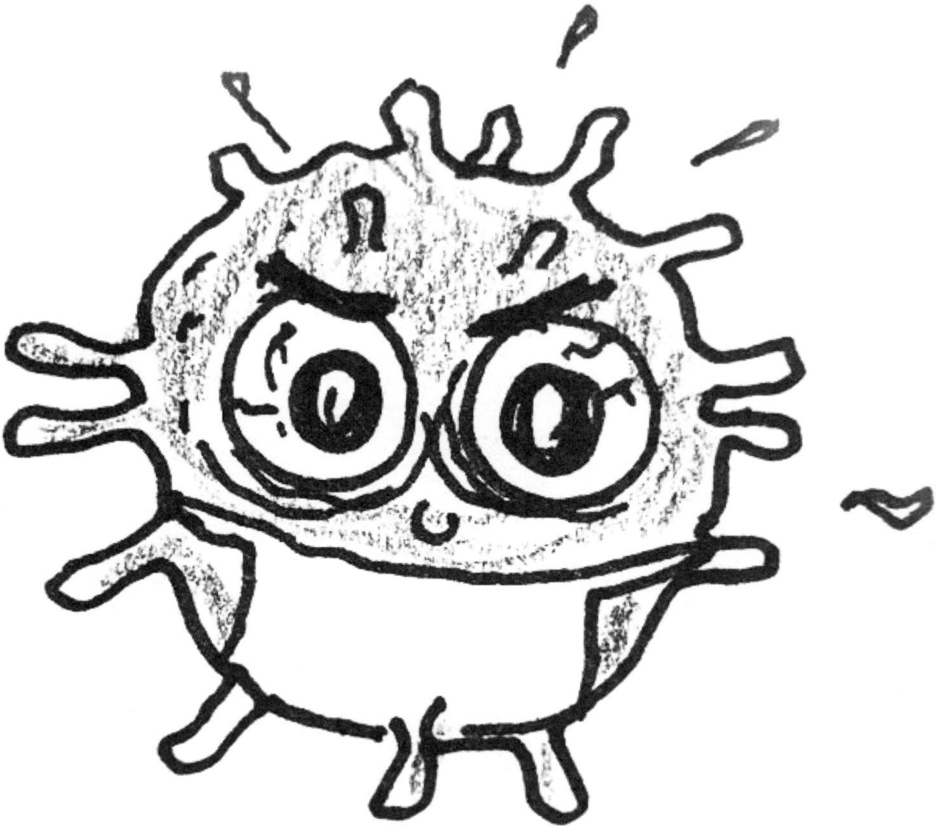

What I Didn't Do in Lockdown

by Yasmine Ollerenshaw - age 15

Chasing a wanted criminal all the way to jail;
More like running after my brother in the damp garden.
Feeding a pack of snarling foxes.
Well, actually giving food to my dogs.
Stroking ancient silks in a historic temple;
Instead, I hugged my old baby clothes.
Staring at the Mona Lisa – that would be awesome -
But instead, I sat watching TV.
Sailing in the ferocious waves of the sea – I wish –
Although I did hear the thunder from my window.
All the amazing things I could have done.
But even better than all of the above
Is spending time with family.

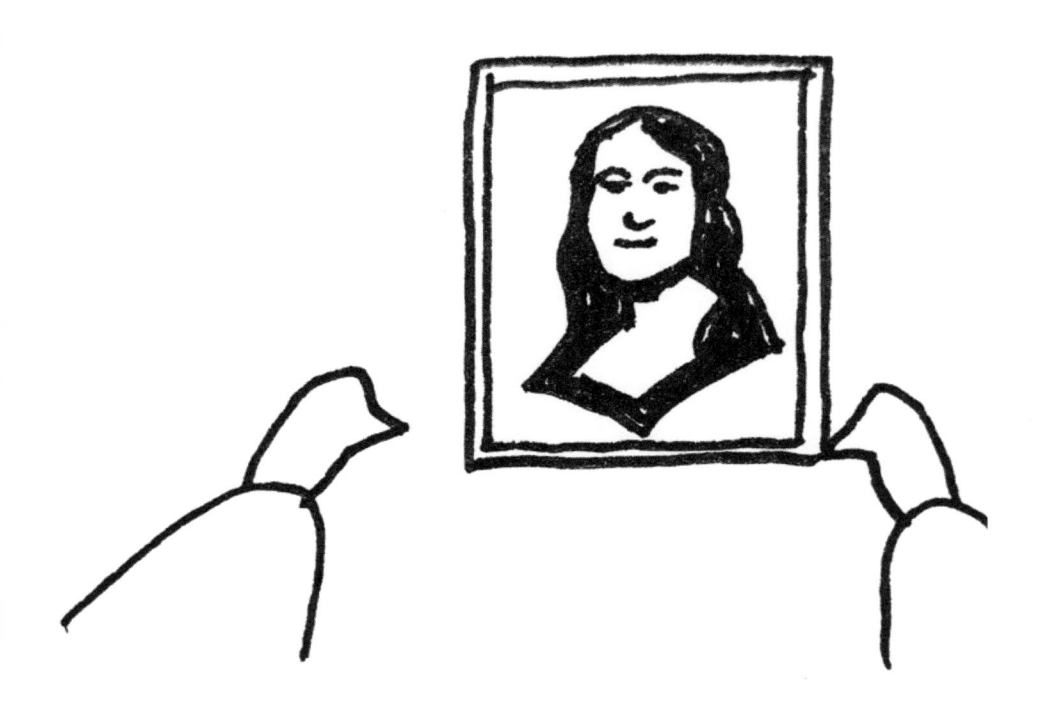

Days Upon Days Slip Away

by Tamisha Newell - age 16

It feels like the world's making us pay
For those mistakes we've all made.
But this is a time of need,
Parents with mouths to feed.
People are coming together
For the first time in forever.

We thank the NHS
For working with all of this stress.
The pandemic sweeping us off our feet,
People we can no longer meet.
Everyone's missing the human connection
And the feeling of affection.
But this is something that will go away,
If in their houses people stay.

Days upon days slipping away.

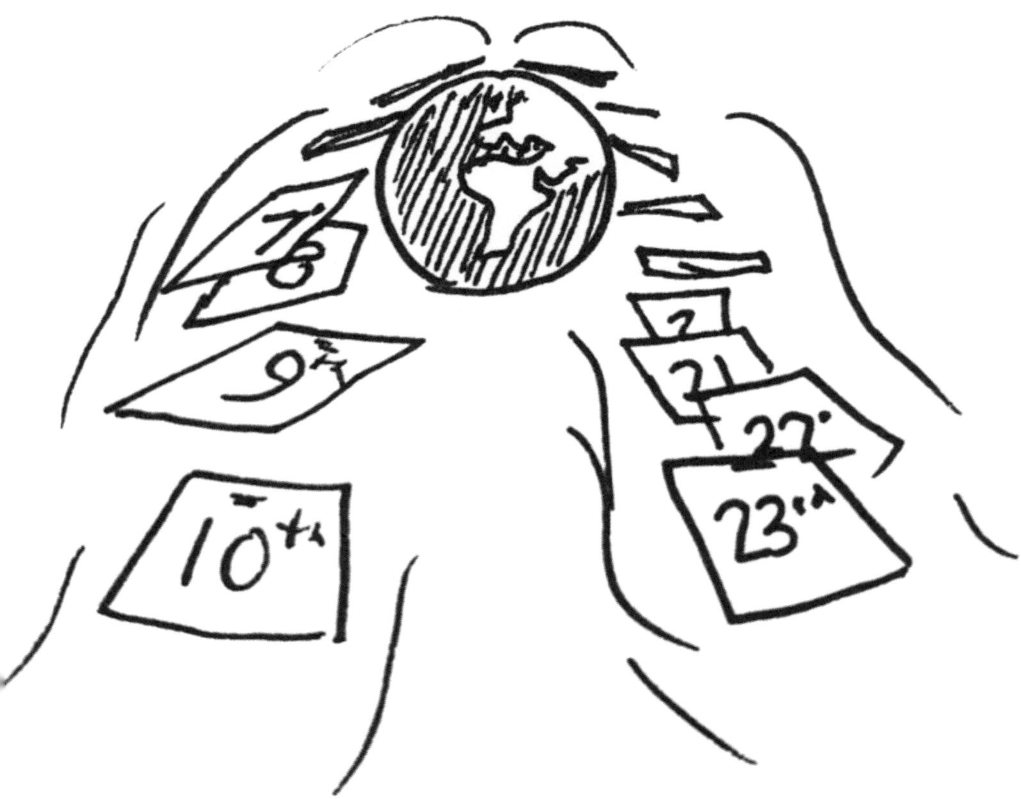
7/8
9th
10th
2
21
22
23rd

The Unravelling Thoughts

by Deekshita Bathula – age 15

The silence feels uncertain,
The emptiness a sin.
The world has paused without consent,
And the birds and their chirping feel constant.

The tar is smooth and unending,
The sidewalk ruled by the ignored,
The eerie tranquillity of the winds.
How unnatural it is to behave
Restrained.

On these days, I close my eyes and travel
Through all the places I have ever seen.
Scents and sounds unravel.
Grateful for the time of open borders,
As memories turn into dreams without orders
To the magical past I bow,
To the upcoming future I work.

Feeling like a bird in a cage,
Filled with unease.
The planet I never thanked enough,
The moments I never had time for.
Life doesn't run as it used to.
We are in fear, we are in hope.
Collectively we stand,
Letting a new way begin.

Stay Home

by Laila Emmett – age 13

Stay at home everyone.
Wash your hands thoroughly
If you cough
All the time.
Feeling hot?
Stay inside,

You might have caught the coronavirus.
So stay inside and save lives,
Contain your germs so you don't let
Others die.

I'm feeling like a sinner;
I went out with my friends and there
Were more than two.
I said she's not standing two
Metres away from you.
Now I'm feeling slightly bad and
Very guilty.
Should have stayed inside and watched
More TV.

Despite All the Sadness

by Lauren Irons– age 13

Although the sky is grey
And the clouds still cry their tears,
Rainbows still appear
In windows of hope
Throughout the year.

And despite this time of loneliness
Where isolation closes in,
The birds still sing their merry song
Morning and evening.

And although the streets are silent,
And the roads are bare of use,
The flowers still bloom
In colours of happiness
To cheer those sad of loneliness.

And despite the schools being empty,
Like a blank page in a book,
Education still goes on
In this new technological way
Of the twenty-first century,
Of today.

Families are further apart,
But still closer than ever before.
And people have more time
To do things that they've wanted to
For a very long time before.

But the tide still comes in
Before going back out.
And the wind still swirls around,
And our delicate planet
Will keep spinning around.

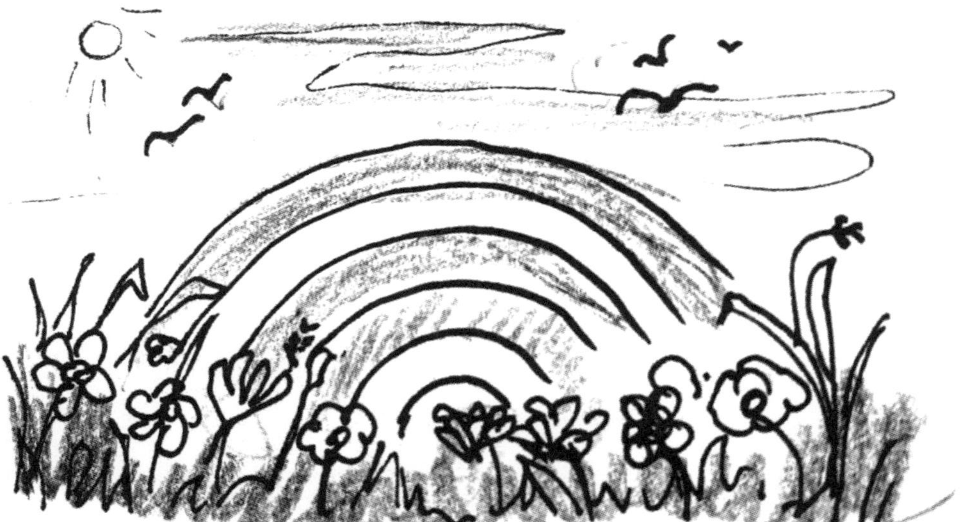

Lockdown Pain

by Donna Craig – Teacher

My experience was one of shock,
When I ordered my shopping and found a block.
I called customer services, but they too
Were out of the office, so what could I do?
The butcher, the baker, florist and club,
All shut down, including the pub.
No toilet rolls, flour or hand gel in sight,
Causing such arguments, even a fight.
I called the dentist when my tooth fell out,
But they too were not about.
Family shielding,
Birthdays not celebrating,
Weddings delayed
And people dismayed.
The virus spread at such a speed,
Even my daughter couldn't escape its greed.
Lockdown was a bit of a pain,
So I am very relieved everything is open again.

Stuck Inside

by Ruby Hoath– age 13

In this difficult time.
Standing alone.
The rose,
And I'm just like it –
Petals falling with the breeze,
Sharp thorns ready to strike enemies,
Feeling protected.

On the inside and out,
Love is shown.
However,
It feels unwanted.
And as much as it tries,
It can't be noticed.

Stuck inside.
Unable to see others,
Unable to leave,
Unable to work,
Unable to travel,
In this desolate time.

As the autumn turns to winter,
Unseen from prying eyes,
The seed hides below the earth,
Ready to come again next summer,
To show how we fought through.

Now read it backwards.

You Called

by Miami Mae Holness – age 13

The ship was bobbing up and down in the salty water,
The waves sizzled as they hit the side.
I looked at my ma and her eyes swelled with pride.

She took my hand and we walked to the line.
The warm island air around me filled up with the smell of the ocean's brine.

We stepped onto the deck,
As ma looked around to check
If leaving Jamaica was the right choice to make.

The days went on.
The journey was perilous and long,
As I watched the Caribbean sun disappear.

My ma shook me awake and someone let out a cheer,
"Hengland! Wi finally ere!"

I skipped my feet,
Left, right,
With excitement as we climbed down the stairs onto the cobbled pavement.

As the sun peeked through the miserable London sky,
It revealed a smart suit and a tie.

It was pa waiting for ma and I.
When he saw us, the two corners of his lips curled up toward the sun.

He picked me up in his muscled arms
And spun me around like a plane,
And everything was peaceful as we were all together again.

The sun was veiled by the clouds,
As we barged through the bustling crowds.
That's when I realised life would never be the same.

England, you called, and we came.

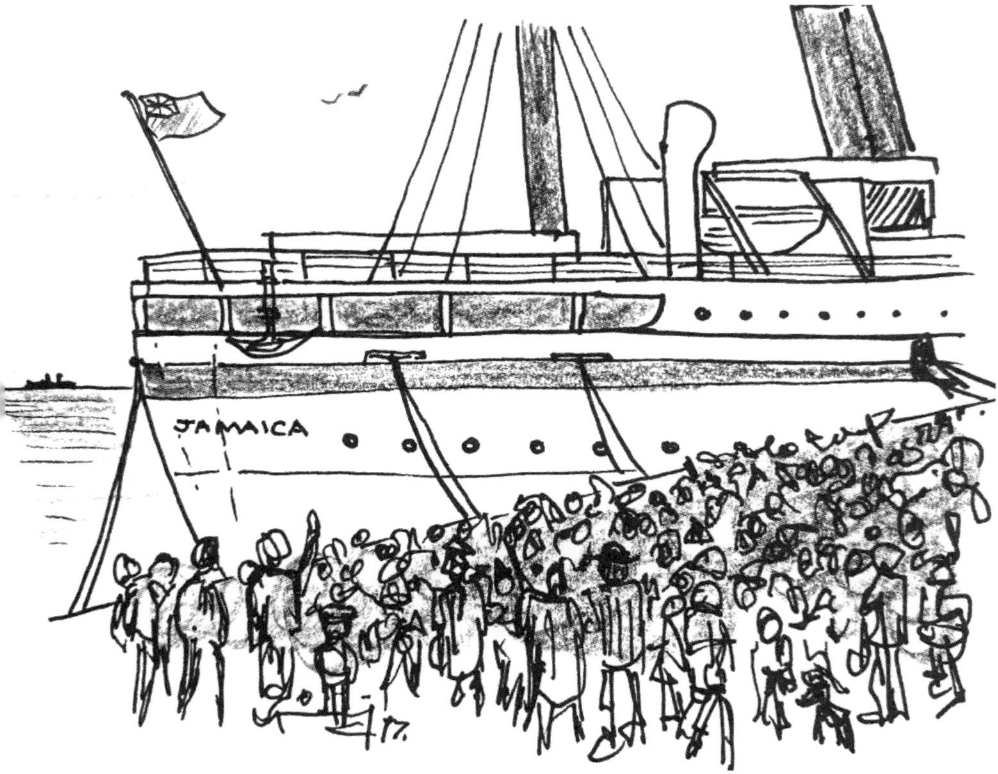
JAMAICA

Quarantine Adventures

by Charlotte Eliza Gunning - age 10

In lockdown I've had lots of fun,
And the fact that normality has not won.
It has given us opportunities to spend bonding time with our family.
And hopefully, at the end of all this,
We can give lockdown a goodbye kiss.
Thank you, key workers, for keeping us safe,
And I hope you never ever see another coronavirus case.
We are so lucky that we have technology,
And when we are home, we study home-school biology.
Online classes and daily walks.
My mum is getting fed-up of me - talk, talk, talk!
But we have to make fun of the free times we have now,
Because when normality comes back around
Never ever will we hear again of lockdown!

Sad

by Amira Collins – age 15

Who knew people like me could benefit from a lockdown?
There are no people to perform in front of when you're out,
And when I say perform, I don't mean a show,
But the facade of pretending to be okay, when you're actually feeling low.
On one side it's freeing,
On the other it's sad
To see how most of the time my mood is actually bad
Or sad,
But rarely glad,
But never mad.
I don't know what I've learned from this experience,
But the part of me that feels emotions sure ain't gonna miss this.

I Would

by Violet Drabble – age 15

I would go out with my friends,
But I never quite get round to it.
It seems that the slowest clock in existence is moving too fast for me.
I can see the days run past me,
Like glimpses of a fever dream from a distant night.

I would call them more often.
I long to chat until midnight and laugh until I can no longer breathe,
But it never, never feels quite the same when I can't reach out and touch;
You feel so distant.

I would live my life 'like a teenager',
Like the characters in my favourite films.
But my movie's been put on pause
And I'm just waiting for the audience to turn it on again.

I would try that little bit harder,
But I'm losing my zest for life and it's taking a while to get it back.
I'm almost counting, wishing away the days until things go back to 'normal'.
But what if normal never comes?

I would look forward to all the good things to come after it all,
But I can't, wondering when exactly that day will arrive.
And if it ever does,
Do I even want this to end?
I've gotten so used to it all that I'd rather just sit in the pool of my sorrows
Than make the effort to get out of it.

Lockdown

by Abi England – age 7

Summer days in the paddling pool.
I go online for virtual school.
I'm happy at home, so it's not all bad.
We're having fun and no one's sad.

Locked up, stocked up,
A country in shock, but
Loving having lockdown at home.

Watching TV is super fun,
I watch it once my work is done.
The Wizards of Waverly Place is the best,
I can't wait to watch the rest.

Locked up, stocked up,
A country in shock, but
Loving having lockdown at home.

My dad and I planted lots of veg
In a patch we built by the garden hedge.
Clapping outside for the NHS,
Drawing rainbows of support, they are the best.

School

by Amber Zaman – age 8

No to school,
No to education,
No to lessons,
And using our imagination.
No to waving goodbye to my parents at the school gates.
No to snacks and pizza on plastic plates.
No to seeing my friends
In the classroom or playground.
No to swim club, football or dancing around.

Keyworker children can go to school.
For them it's a slightly different rule,
But only if they cannot be cared for at home.
Then they are better at school and not alone.
Shielding children must stay inside.
Well away from the virus, they must hide.
The phased re-opening of schools is put on hold.
A government statement that was just too bold.
Two… metres… apart… what is going on?
School paused, home-schooling instead, my routine totally gone.

Hey!

by Georgina Agate – age 13

Are you there?
Just checking in,
Again.
I know times are hard,
I know you're pretty lonely.
I wanted to call just to ask,

Are you ok?
Have you been out,
Gone on a walk?
What are you up to
When in your house?
I know it's overwhelming.

"Stay in."
"You could die."
I know it's true,
But, I have to admit,
It's scary.

I guess I just wanna say
I miss you
And that I hope you're ok.
So call me, because

I'm just checking in.

Coronavirus

by Katie Battams - age 11

Our holidays cancelled.
One walk through the trees.
Sitting at home,
Can't travel overseas.

Can't go to school,
Our lives on hold.
Won't see our friends.
All the toilet roll sold.

Out on our bikes,
So much gardening to do.
Trying new crafts each day
With paper and glue.

Everything is boring.
Our lives filled with hope.
Always washing our hands
With water and soap.

Although it seems slow,
We will get through.
And thank you NHS
For everything you do.

Lockdown

by Sophie Baker– age 13

I'm stuck in this never-ending loop,
My waking hours feel like I'm dreaming.
The loud words rushing around inside my head,
Like wind on a stormy day.
It is never-ending.
My dreams feel so real,
Like none of this has ever happened.
Everything's playing over and over in my head, like a broken record.
I'm stuck in this never-ending loop.

Heroes

by Cohan Burnham - age 15

Sitting at the kitchen table,
Mum is teaching us.
All you can hear
Is the fridge's buzz.

My sister's driving me up the wall,
She's totally insane!
But mum is just ignoring it
And sipping on champagne.

Dad is working in my room,
So mum is cooking tea.
She doesn't usually do this,
So say a prayer for me.

Dad has finished for the day
And flops down on the couch.
But then he has a moan at me
And tells me not to slouch.

Standing on the doorstep,
Clapping in the night.
The neighbours out as well,
What an awesome sight.

As I lay in bed at night,
I dream of armadillos.
In the morning I watch the news
And salute our British *heroes*.

Change

by Rachel Pugh – age 13

It started when school came to an end
Without so much as a goodbye from a friend.
Everyone stuck at home
With no freedom to roam.
Meeting friends on Zoom,
Sprucing up our virtual room.
Some people starting fitness,
While others try to avoid the illness.
Everything changing,
All lives rearranging.
Appreciating friends more,
Waiting for them to knock at the door.
Starting bubbles with the ones you've missed,
Continuing to persist.
Black lives matter, the most important message,
Teaching the whole world a needed lesson.
Needed change coming through,
Refusing to be subdued.
That's my lockdown message for you.
Thanks for reading my debut.

A New Normal

by Jessica McAndrew Woods - Teacher

Bright blue sky,
Grass freshly cut.
Welcoming students and staff
To cheer at the finish line,
A day that never happened.

Email after email,
Coffee after coffee.
Zoom calls, family calls and WhatsApp groups
Checking welfare, mental health and safety.
Told to stay at home.

A building made for a thousand or more,
With thirty inside
Day after day.
Signing in,
Passing buildings with chains on the doors,
Equipment wrapped in hazard tape.
Confined to the library,
Learning remotely.

And as September rolls around
With its staggered entrances and lunchtimes,
We stand behind the line taped to the classroom floor,
Instructing: sanitise and distance,
Stay in your bubble.
Craving connection
And embracing a new normal.

Lockdown Poem

by Ayla Cheesman – age 12

Lockdown has been hard for all of us.
It's been hard for the grandparents who can't give you hugs.
It's been hard for the people who have got the bug.
It's been hard for the kids who can't touch their friends.
It's been hard for everyone, including best friends.
Touching things is a hazard right now,
So please keep your hands to yourself, I don't know how.
Wear a mask, be safe from the virus.
All of this is a very big crisis.
Keep up your hopes and start dreaming,
All of this will start to have a meaning.

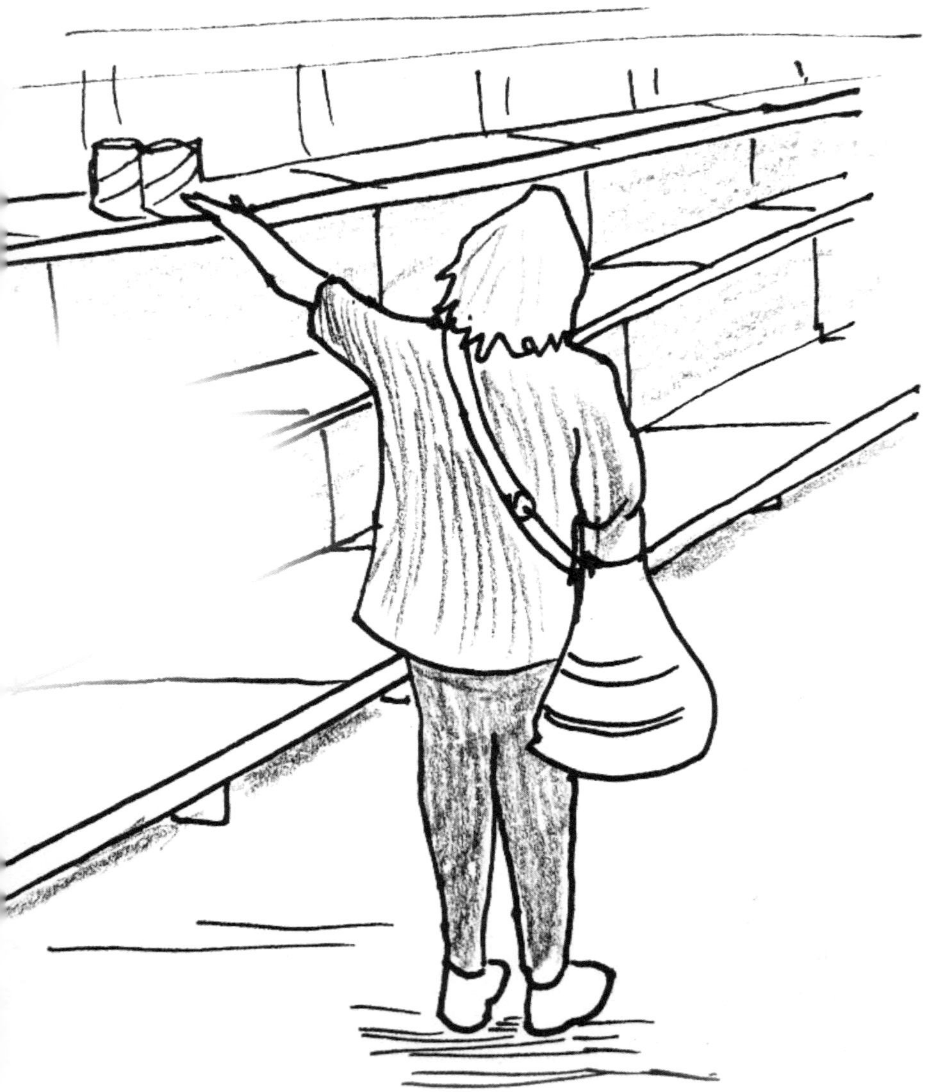

When It's Over

by Ania Mahi-Moutih – age 13

When this is over
May we nevermore
Take for granted:
A handshake with a stranger,
Full shelves of food at Sainsbury's,
Interactions with neighbours,
The school rush each morning,
A crowded shopping centre,
Coffee at a café,
Each deep breath,
A tiresome Monday,
Life itself.

When this is over
May we treasure
The simple things,
The key workers,
Who have selflessly
Put their lives in front of ours,
A breath of fresh air,
And that these hard times are finally over.

Locked Down, This Town

by Olive Felstead – age 12

Locked down,
This town.

I cannot bare it any more,
I simply must go out the door

To see my friends and family
Or to buy groceries.

Locked down,
This town.

Face coverings,
People suffering,

Two metres apart,
Being trapped behind a bar.

Locked down,
This town.

Shops closed,
Everything put on hold.

Birthdays at home,
Left feeling all alone.

Locked down,
This town.

I wait for the end,
But time seems to endlessly extend.

Locked down,
This town.

Kindness

by Gabriel Richardson – age 12

Kindness is being human and accepting the people around us,
Understanding that we should be nice and not make a fuss.
Kindness is making the most out of our situations,
Taking the lead and having inspiration.
Kindness is looking out for others,
Our family, friends, sisters, and brothers.

Rays of sunshine, nice long baths,
Our best memories where we can sit back and laugh.

Kindness, a straight path, a way to get through the day,
Then come home on a hot day in May.
Kindness is being open, honest
To those that we might have promised.

Overall
Kindness is forgiving, as it is easy to keep a grudge,
Yet harder to let one go.

Quarantine Time

by Nihal Bathula - age 11

The lonely, whistling wind,
The calmly risen sun.
The blossoming flowers,
The healing of nature.

The fun family games I play.
The amazing memories I make.
The wavering future,
The unpredictability of life.

The tireless nights the doctors had,
The precious lives they saved.
The more I think,
The prouder I feel.
Together we stand.

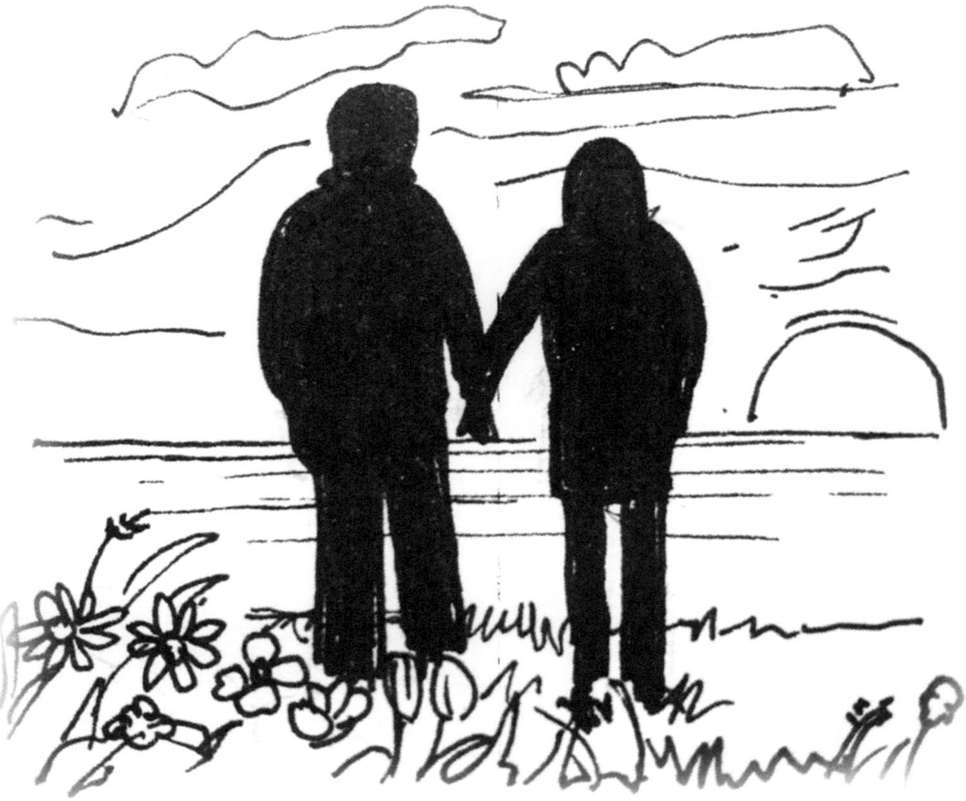

We All Stayed at Home

by Isabella Hickman – age 16

We all stayed at home
To help the NHS cope.
Fears ran deep,
But there was always hope.

In times of difficulty
Community is what you need,
And during the pandemic
The vulnerable we helped to feed.

It's easy to forget what's important
Until you stop and take a step back.
When we begin to take a step back,
For the art of caring we get the knack.

Some people played games,
While others read.
Some people learnt yoga skills
And baked banana bread.

Most took the time to reflect
And once again learnt how to connect.

The Moments We Miss

by Scout Wyatt – age 13

It's funny how the moments we miss,
Those moments of bliss,
Are the moments we would not think twice about before.
But now they are gone
And it's their absence we cannot ignore.

It's the simple things –
Stopping off, passing by, dropping in,
A quick cup of tea for which you'll cave,
Though now we must suffice with merely a wave.

It's everyday life
Swept before our eyes.
Reality has become insanity.
Normal becomes paranormal.
Who could predict it?
Would you believe it?

It's the going outside,
The eating out, the weekly shop,
The pit stops.
It's now the doubt, the worry, the not knowing
When we'll get out.

Silence

by Elaine Brandon – Teacher

Silence is golden (that's what they say).
Well you come and try it, day after day,
In a place that's so usually noisy and vibrant,
But is now like a ghost town, drowning in quiet.

It started with media hype back in March.
'Close the schools!' came the shout, and yes, by and large
We agreed with the logic behind the decision,
But had no real idea of the size of the mission,
To educate, care for, and connect with our students
Who were sitting alone, behind their computers,
Wanting to study, listen and learn,
Waiting for us to reach them at home.

Broadband was buzzing all over the nation,
Hosting meetings, hangouts, and endless communication,
As teachers everywhere set out to learn
The basics of Google Classroom and Zoom.

We carried on going to work in our school,
Where, honestly, most days I felt like a fool
Being challenged by new tech and app innovation.
Oh, God! This was such a bad situation!
I smiled even though I was crying inside -
Where were the kids upon whom I'd relied
To show me the ins and the outs of these gadgets?
It seemed as though school life was laying in ashes.

The roads were quiet, the air was still,
The whole situation was completely surreal.
And all the time the building stood waiting
For the day that its heart would again start pulsating
With the steady rhythm of its purpose and soul,
The children – who are what make it a whole.

Coronavirus

by Zachary Symonds – age 13

Coronavirus, you've taken so much,
You've concealed our loved ones away from our touch.
You've cancelled our plans and trips away.
We are all stuck at home, where for now we must stay.

School has been postponed, our lessons online.
It was ok at first, but now it's lost its shine.
We miss our friends and our daily routine,
Chats in the playground and laughs in the canteen.

We will do it forever, if that's what it takes,
Because coronavirus has threatened the highest of stakes.
We will stay inside and follow the rules,
We will draw rainbows, bake cakes and do some home-school.

We don't really care that life is on hold,
As when this is all over, our family we'll hold.
When lockdown is raised and we're allowed out,
We'll appreciate our freedom without a doubt.
We'll be proud of this time when the world went to sleep
To keep loved ones safe. Until then, hugs we'll keep.

Since Lockdown Began

by Thea Markus - age 12

The day begins like every other:
Stood by the window looking out,
Then head downstairs for a cup of tea
And an early morning workout.

Some are working harder
Than they've ever worked before.
Some wait for a parcel
To be delivered to their door.

Later on there's entertainment,
Frozen screens on Zoom,
Sat taking part in quizzes
In your virtual living room.

Empty streets, empty shelves,
Face masks worn outside.
Restaurants are closed,
But takeaways, they will provide.

We all applaud the NHS
While banging pots and pans,
Thinking about how long it's been
Since lockdown began.

Trapped Inside

by Josh Crabbe – age 12

We're trapped inside, looking out,
There's never any people about.

We're trapped inside with sisters and brothers,
Stuck with our dads and our mothers.

We're trapped inside with home-schooling time,
Doing work in books and online.

We're trapped inside eating dad's experimental meals.
The dogs need walking, they're yapping like seals.

We're trapped inside, not allowed to see our friends.
But we'll have a party when lockdown ends.

We trapped inside while key workers work hard,
Keeping the world two meters apart.

We're trapped inside, months going by,
Just hoping the economy doesn't die.

Trapped inside, using Zoom meetings and video chats.
Let's call our friends and family perhaps.

Trapped inside, just trapped inside.
Thank you NHS for keeping us alive.

Not Over Yet

by Michael Bourton - Poet & Illustrator

When I wrote the virus poems,
I thought they'd have an end.
Sadly I was mistaken,
Hard to comprehend

When this is going to finish,
When masks will be no more.
For now I have to remember
When I walk out the door

To pick a mask to go out
To the shops and coffee bar.
I keep them on a special hook,
I keep them in my car.

Strange how much we focus
On what mask to wear.
New fashions change the way we are,
Our living virus gear.

I miss your smile so much my friend
When I greet you in the street.
One day I hope for masks no more
And hugs for when we meet.

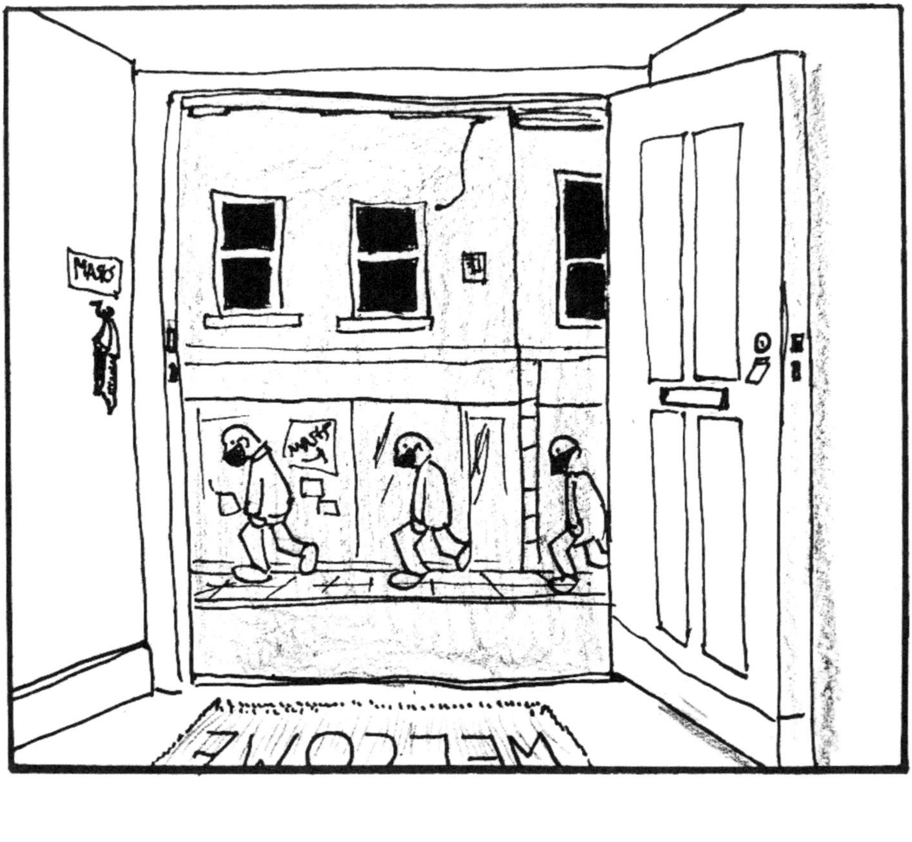

Jenny Agutter
Actress & Patron of Children's Literature Festivals

Dr Stephen Fear
Entrepreneur & Businessman & Patron of Children's Literature Festivals

Michael Bradley
Musician & Patron of Children's Literature Festivals

Christina Gabbitas
Author, Voice Artist & Founder of Children's Literature Festivals

PC Stephen Croshaw
Police Officer, Warwickshire Police

PC Russ Massie
Police Officer, Thames Valley Police, Violence Reduction Unit

Ali Jeremy
Director of Communications & Engagement at The Royal Parks

Donavan Christopher
Poet & Author

Andy Seed
Poet & Author

Sue Hardy-Dawson
Poet & Ullustrator

Rebecca Thomas
Translator & Editor

David Niven
Safeguarding Expert

Kirsty Tock
Police Officer, Humberside Police

Conrad Burdekin
Poet

Alex White
Author

Michael Bourton
Poet & Illustrator

Salma Zaman
Author & Bollywood Dance Teacher

Matt Goodfellow
Poet & Educator

Ann Marie Christian
Safeguarding Expert & Author

Julie Fulton
Author

Dom Conlon
Author & Poet

Hilary Robinson
Author

Ursula Hurst
Illustrator

Julie Ann Douglas
Poet & Author

Lauren Oldacre
Creative Writer